# HERSHEY'S®

## *Holiday Favorites*

# HERSHEY'S®

## Holiday Favorites

Publications International, Ltd.

Favorite Brand Name Recipes at www.fbnr.com

HERSHEY'S, KISSES, MINI KISSES, MINI CHIPS, HEATH, REESE'S and SPECIAL DARK are registered trademarks of Hershey Foods Corporation, Hershey, PA 17033.
MOUNDS is a licensed trademark of Hershey Foods Corporation, Hershey, PA 17033.

Photography, *except* that on page 6, by Stephen Hamilton Photographics, Inc., Chicago
**Photographers:** Eric Coughlin, Tate Hunt
**Photographers' Assistant:** Ray Barrera
**Prop Stylist:** Paula Walters
**Food Stylists:** Kathy Joy, Walter Moeller
**Assistant Food Stylist:** Thomas Sherman

**Pictured on the front cover** *(clockwise from top left):* Chilled Raspberry Cheesecake *(page 56),* Peanut Blossoms *(page 36),* Hershey's Chocolate Peppermint Roll *(page 46)* and Peanut Butter Fudge Brownie Bars *(page 68).*

**Pictured on the back cover** *(left to right):* Chocolate KISSES® Mousse *(page 32)* and Fudgey Coconut Clusters *(page 10).*

ISBN-13: 978-1-4127-2451-7
ISBN-10: 1-4127-2451-1

Manufactured in China.

8 7 6 5 4 3 2 1

**Microwave Cooking:** Microwave ovens vary in wattage. Use the cooking times as guidelines and check for doneness before adding more time.

# Table of **Contents**

# HERSHEY'S®

# New Traditions with Hershey's®

## THE TRADITION CONTINUES

Milton S. Hershey was born in 1857 near Derry Church, Pa., and began his confectionery career as an apprentice to a candymaker in Lancaster, Pa. After struggling to establish a successful company in various locations across the nation, he returned to Lancaster in 1886 to found the business that established his candy-making reputation, the Lancaster Caramel Company.

In 1893, Mr. Hershey became fascinated with German chocolate-making machinery on exhibit at the World's Columbian Exposition in Chicago and purchased the equipment for his Lancaster plant. He soon began producing his own chocolate coatings for caramels, and in 1894 the Hershey Chocolate Company was born as a subsidiary of his Lancaster caramel business. In addition to chocolate coatings, Mr. Hershey produced breakfast cocoa, sweet chocolate, and baking chocolate.

After selling his caramel business to concentrate on chocolate, Mr. Hershey returned to his birthplace and began construction in 1903 on what is now the world's largest chocolate manufacturing plant, located in a town now known as Hershey, Pa.

## A NEW AMERICAN CLASSIC

In 1907, Mr. Hershey re-shaped the candy industry, introducing a brand-new way to enjoy delicious Hershey's chocolate: Hershey's Kisses®BRAND Milk Chocolates. These scrumptious treats soon became his signature product, and today they are synonymous with his company and his town.

Though Hershey's Kisses®BRAND chocolates are most commonly seen disappearing from candy bowls, they have become increasingly popular baking ingredients as well, and we understand why. They look and taste great—the perfect way to top your favorite recipes!

It's hard to believe, but beginning in 2004, Hershey's Kisses®BRAND chocolates are even better for baking. Kisses®BRAND chocolates are now unwrapped and recipe-ready. They're more convenient, making baking more fun and less work. Looks like we've unwrapped the secret to wonderful desserts!

Since the 1920s, Hershey's Kitchens has created mouth-watering recipes for spectacular cakes, irresistible cookies, and much more. These recipes have featured the best Hershey's ingredients, been easy to prepare, and created smiles at every family function.

The tradition continues with this edition of "Hershey's Holiday Favorites." Read on for many classic favorites, including an entire chapter dedicated to Hershey's Kisses®BRAND chocolates. When your family tastes our recipes and our products, they are sure to agree that Hershey makes mealtimes a little sweeter.

# Baking with Hershey's

## BAKING MADE DELICIOUSLY EASY

We're proud to offer these delicious Hershey's baking ingredients for all your holiday—and everyday—baking needs. With such a variety, making dessert a memorable occasion has never been easier or more certain!

Unsweetened
Cocoa

Dutch Processed
Cocoa

Semi-Sweet Chocolate Chips

Unwrapped
Hershey's Kisses®BRAND Baking
Pieces

Milk Chocolate Chips

Mini Kisses® Milk Chocolates

Special Dark® Chips

Mini Chips™ Semi-Sweet
Chocolates

Reese's® Peanut Butter
Chips

Reese's® Peanut Butter &
Milk Chocolate Chips

Heath® Milk Chocolate
Toffee Bits

Heath® Bits 'O Brickle®
Toffee Bits

Butterscotch Chips

Premier White Chips

Cinnamon Chips

Raspberry Chips

Semi-Sweet Chocolate for
Baking

Mint Chocolate Chips

Unsweetened Chocolate for
Baking

Mounds® Sweetened
Coconut Flakes

# cookies

## Fudgey Coconut Clusters

*Makes about 2½ dozen cookies*

- 5⅓ cups MOUNDS® Sweetened Coconut Flakes
- 1 can (14 ounces) sweetened condensed milk (not evaporated milk)
- ⅔ cup HERSHEY'S Cocoa
- ¼ cup (½ stick) butter, melted
- 2 teaspoons vanilla extract
- 1½ teaspoons almond extract
  HERSHEY'S MINI KISSES®BRAND Milk Chocolates or candied cherry halves (optional)

**1.** Heat oven to 350°F. Line cookie sheets with aluminum foil; generously grease foil with vegetable shortening.

**2.** Combine coconut, sweetened condensed milk, cocoa, melted butter, vanilla and almond extract in large bowl; mix well. Drop by rounded tablespoons onto prepared cookie sheets.

**3.** Bake 9 to 11 minutes or just until set; press 3 milk chocolates or candied cherry halves in center of each cookie, if desired. Immediately remove cookies to wire rack and cool completely.

**VARIATION:** Chocolate Chip Macaroons: Omit melted butter and cocoa; stir together other ingredients. Add 1 cup HERSHEY'S MINI CHIPS™ Semi-Sweet Chocolate Chips. Bake 9 to 11 minutes or just until set. Immediately remove to wire racks and cool completely.

Fudgey Coconut Clusters

# cookies

## Reduced-Sugar Chocolate Chip Cookies

*Makes 3 dozen cookies*

- ½ **cup (1 stick) butter or margarine, softened**
- ¼ **cup sugar**
- ½ **cup measure-for-measure sugar substitute**
- 1 **egg**
- 1 **teaspoon vanilla extract**
- 1 **cup all-purpose flour**
- 3 **tablespoons HERSHEY'S Cocoa or HERSHEY'S Dutch Processed Cocoa**
- ½ **teaspoon baking soda**
- ⅛ **teaspoon salt**
- 2 **tablespoons skim milk**
- ⅓ **cup HERSHEY'S MINI CHIPS™ Semi-Sweet Chocolate Chips**

**1.** Heat oven to 375°F.

**2.** Beat butter, sugar and sugar substitute with electric mixer on medium speed in medium bowl until well blended. Add egg and vanilla; beat well. Stir together flour, cocoa, baking soda and salt; add alternately with milk to butter mixture, beating until well blended. Stir in mini chocolate chips. Drop by teaspoons onto ungreased cookie sheet.

**3.** Bake 7 to 9 minutes or just until set. Remove to wire rack and cool completely.

Reduced-Sugar Chocolate Chip Cookies

## Chewy Drizzled Cinnamon Chip Cookies

*Makes about 5 dozen cookies*

- ¾ cup (1½ sticks) butter or margarine, softened
- 1 cup packed light brown sugar
- ¼ cup light corn syrup
- 1 egg
- 1⅔ cups (10-ounce package) HERSHEY'S Cinnamon Chips, divided
- 2½ cups all-purpose flour
- 2 teaspoons baking soda
- ¼ teaspoon salt
- 1 cup finely ground pecans or walnuts
- 1½ teaspoons shortening (do not use butter, margarine, spread or oil)

**1.** Beat butter and brown sugar with electric mixer on medium speed in large bowl until fluffy. Add corn syrup and egg; mix well.

**2.** Place 1 cup cinnamon chips in microwave-safe bowl. Microwave on HIGH (100%) 1 minute or just until chips are melted when stirred. Stir melted chips into butter mixture.

**3.** Stir together flour, baking soda and salt; add to cinnamon chips mixture, beating with electric mixer just until blended. Cover; refrigerate dough about 1 hour or until firm enough to handle.

**4.** Heat oven to 350°F. Shape dough into 1-inch balls; roll in nuts, lightly pressing nuts into dough. Place on ungreased cookie sheet.

**5.** Bake 8 to 10 minutes or until golden around edges. Cool slightly. Remove to wire rack and cool completely.

**6.** Place remaining ⅔ cup cinnamon chips and shortening in small microwave-safe bowl. Microwave on HIGH 1 minute or until chips are melted and mixture is smooth when stirred. Drizzle evenly over cooled cookies.

## HERSHEY'S Double Chocolate Mint Cookies

*Makes about 2¹/₂ dozen cookies*

- ²/₃ **cup butter or margarine, softened**
- 1 **cup sugar**
- 1 **egg**
- 1 **teaspoon vanilla extract**
- 1 **cup all-purpose flour**
- ¹/₂ **cup HERSHEY'S Cocoa**
- ¹/₂ **teaspoon baking soda**
- ¹/₄ **teaspoon salt**
- 1²/₃ **cups (10-ounce package) HERSHEY'S Mint Chocolate Chips**

**1.** Heat oven to 350°F.

**2.** Beat butter and sugar with electric mixer on medium speed in large bowl until creamy. Add egg and vanilla; beat well. Stir together flour, cocoa, baking soda and salt; gradually add to butter mixture, beating well. Stir in mint chocolate chips. Drop by rounded teaspoons onto ungreased cookie sheet.

**3.** Bake 8 to 9 minutes or just until set; do not overbake. Cool slightly. Remove to wire rack and cool completely.

## REESE'S® Peanut Butter and Milk Chocolate Chip Tassies

*Makes 3 dozen cookies*

- ¾ cup (1½ sticks) butter, softened
- 1 package (3 ounces) cream cheese, softened
- 1½ cups all-purpose flour
- ¾ cup sugar, divided
- 1 egg, lightly beaten
- 2 tablespoons butter or margarine, melted
- ¼ teaspoon lemon juice
- ¼ teaspoon vanilla extract
- 1¾ cups (11-ounce package) REESE'S® Peanut Butter and Milk Chocolate Chips, divided
- 2 teaspoons shortening (do not use butter, margarine, spread or oil)

**1.** Beat ¾ cup butter and cream cheese with electric mixer on medium speed in medium bowl until well blended; add flour and ¼ cup sugar, beating until well blended. Cover; refrigerate about 1 hour or until dough is firm. Shape dough into 1-inch balls; press balls onto bottoms and up sides of 36 small muffin cups (1¾ inches in diameter).

**2.** Heat oven to 350°F. Combine egg, remaining ½ cup sugar, melted butter, lemon juice and vanilla in small bowl; stir until smooth. Set aside ⅓ cup chips; add remainder to egg mixture. Evenly fill muffin cups with chip mixture.

**3.** Bake 20 to 25 minutes or until filling is set and lightly browned. Cool completely; remove from pan to wire rack.

**4.** Combine reserved ⅓ cup chips and shortening in small microwave-safe bowl. Microwave at HIGH (100%) 30 seconds; stir. If necessary, microwave additional 15 seconds at a time, stirring after each heating, until chips are melted and mixture is smooth when stirred. Drizzle over tops of tassies.

REESE'S® Peanut Butter and Milk Chocolate Chip Tassies

# cookies

## Buche De Noel Cookies

*Makes about 2½ dozen cookies*

- ⅔ **cup butter or margarine, softened**
- 1 **cup granulated sugar**
- 2 **eggs**
- 2 **teaspoons vanilla extract**
- 2½ **cups all-purpose flour**
- ½ **cup HERSHEY'S Cocoa**
- ½ **teaspoon baking soda**
- ¼ **teaspoon salt**
  - **Mocha Frosting (recipe follows)**
  - **Powdered sugar (optional)**

**1.** Beat butter and sugar with electric mixer on medium speed in large bowl until well blended. Add eggs and vanilla; beat until fluffy. Stir together flour, cocoa, baking soda and salt; gradually add to butter mixture, beating until well blended. Cover; refrigerate dough 1 to 2 hours.

**2.** Heat oven to 350°F. Shape heaping teaspoons of dough into logs about 2½ inches long and ¾ inches in diameter; place on ungreased cookie sheet. Bake 7 to 9 minutes or until set. Cool slightly. Remove to wire rack and cool completely.

**3.** Frost cookies with Mocha Frosting. Using tines of fork, draw lines through frosting to imitate tree bark. Lightly dust with powdered sugar, if desired.

## Mocha Frosting

*Makes about 1⅔ cups frosting*

- 6 **tablespoons butter or margarine, softened**
- 2⅔ **cups powdered sugar**
- ⅓ **cup HERSHEY'S Cocoa**
- 3 **to 4 tablespoons milk**
- 2 **teaspoons powdered instant espresso dissolved in**
  - 1 **teaspoon hot water**
- 1 **teaspoon vanilla extract**

Beat butter with electric mixer on medium speed in medium bowl until creamy. Add powdered sugar and cocoa alternately with milk, dissolved espresso and vanilla, beating to spreadable consistency.

Buche De Noel Cookies

# cookies

## HERSHEY'S SPECIAL DARK® Chocolate Chip Cookies

*Makes about 3½ dozen cookies*

- 6 **tablespoons butter, softened**
- ⅓ **cup butter flavored shortening**
- ½ **cup packed light brown sugar**
- ⅓ **cup granulated sugar**
- 1 **egg**
- 1½ **teaspoons vanilla extract**
- 1¼ **cups all-purpose flour**
- ½ **teaspoon baking soda**
- ½ **teaspoon salt**
- 2 **cups (12-ounce package) HERSHEY'S SPECIAL DARK® Chocolate Chips**
- ¾ **cup chopped nuts (optional)**

**1.** Heat oven to 350°F.

**2.** Beat butter and shortening with electric mixer on medium speed in large bowl until well blended. Add brown sugar and granulated sugar; beat thoroughly. Add egg and vanilla, beating until well blended. Stir together flour, baking soda and salt; gradually beat into butter mixture. Stir in chocolate chips and nuts, if desired. Drop by rounded teaspoons onto ungreased cookie sheet.

**3.** Bake 10 to 12 minutes or until lightly browned. Cool slightly. Remove to wire rack and cool completely.

## Chewy Coconut Oatmeal Drops

*Makes about 5 dozen cookies*

- ¾ cup (1½ sticks) butter or margarine, softened
- ¾ cup granulated sugar
- ¾ cup packed light brown sugar
- 2 eggs
- 1 teaspoon vanilla extract
- 2 cups all-purpose flour
- 1 teaspoon baking soda
- ½ teaspoon salt
- 2 cups **MOUNDS®** Sweetened Coconut Flakes
- 1½ cups quick-cooking or regular rolled oats

**1.** Heat oven to 350°F.

**2.** Beat butter, granulated sugar and brown sugar with electric mixer on medium speed in large bowl until well blended. Beat in eggs and vanilla. Stir together flour, baking soda and salt; add to butter mixture, beating until blended. Stir in coconut and oats (dough will be thick). Drop by teaspoons onto ungreased cookie sheet.

**3.** Bake 8 to 10 minutes or until edges are lightly browned. Cool slightly. Remove to wire rack and cool completely.

## Holiday Double Peanut Butter Fudge Cookies

*Makes about 3½ dozen cookies*

- 1 can (14 ounces) sweetened condensed milk (not evaporated milk)
- ¾ cup REESE'S® Creamy Peanut Butter
- 2 cups all-purpose biscuit baking mix
- 1 teaspoon vanilla extract
- ¾ cup REESE'S® Peanut Butter Chips
- ¼ cup granulated sugar
- ½ teaspoon red colored sugar
- ½ teaspoon green colored sugar

**1.** Heat oven to 375°F.

**2.** Beat sweetened condensed milk and peanut butter with electric mixer on medium speed in large bowl until smooth. Beat in baking mix and vanilla; stir in peanut butter chips. Set aside.

**3.** Stir together granulated sugar and colored sugars in small bowl. Shape dough into 1-inch balls; roll in sugar. Place 2 inches apart on ungreased cookie sheet; flatten slightly with bottom of glass.

**4.** Bake 6 to 8 minutes or until very lightly browned (do not overbake). Cool slightly. Remove to wire rack and cool completely. Store in tightly covered container.

Holiday Double Peanut Butter Fudge Cookies

## Oatmeal Butterscotch Cookies

*Makes about 4 dozen cookies*

- ¾ cup (1½ sticks) butter or margarine, softened
- ¾ cup granulated sugar
- ¾ cup packed light brown sugar
- 2 eggs
- 1 teaspoon vanilla extract
- 1¼ cups all-purpose flour
- 1 teaspoon baking soda
- ½ teaspoon salt
- ½ teaspoon ground cinnamon
- 3 cups quick-cooking or regular rolled oats, uncooked
- 1¾ cups (11-ounce package) HERSHEY'S Butterscotch Chips

**1.** Heat oven to 375°F.

**2.** Beat butter, granulated sugar and brown sugar with electric mixer on medium speed in large bowl until well blended. Add eggs and vanilla; blend thoroughly. Stir together flour, baking soda, salt and cinnamon; gradually add to butter mixture, beating until well blended. Stir in oats and butterscotch chips; mix well. Drop by teaspoons onto ungreased cookie sheet.

**3.** Bake 8 to 10 minutes or until golden brown. Cool slightly. Remove to wire rack and cool completely.

Oatmeal Butterscotch Cookies

# Drizzled Raspberry Crinkles

*Makes about 5 dozen cookies*

- 1⅔ cups (10-ounce package) HERSHEY'S Raspberry Chips, divided
- 1 cup (2 sticks) butter or margarine, softened
- 1 cup packed light brown sugar
- ¾ cup granulated sugar
- 2 eggs
- 1 teaspoon vanilla extract
- 2½ cups all-purpose flour
- ⅓ cup HERSHEY'S Cocoa
- 1 teaspoon baking powder
- 1 teaspoon baking soda
- 1½ teaspoons shortening (do not use butter, margarine, spread or oil)

**1.** Heat oven to 350°F.

**2.** Set aside ½ cup raspberry chips. Place remaining chips in small microwave-safe bowl. Microwave at HIGH (100%) 1 minute or until melted when stirred.

**3.** Beat butter, brown sugar and granulated sugar with electric mixer on medium speed in large bowl until well blended. Add melted chips; beat until well blended. Beat in eggs and vanilla. Stir together flour, cocoa, baking powder and baking soda. Gradually beat into chocolate mixture. Drop by rounded teaspoons onto ungreased cookie sheet.

**4.** Bake 8 to 9 minutes for chewy cookies or 10 to 11 minutes for crisp cookies. Cool slightly. Remove to wire rack and cool completely.

**5.** Place reserved chips and shortening in small microwave-safe bowl. Microwave at HIGH 30 seconds or until chips are melted when stirred. Drizzle over cookies.

# Really Chocolate Chocolate Chip Cookies

*Makes about 5 dozen cookies*

- 6 **tablespoons butter or margarine, softened**
- 6 **tablespoons butter flavored shortening**
- ⅔ **cup packed light brown sugar**
- ½ **cup granulated sugar**
- 2 **eggs**
- 2 **tablespoons milk**
- 2 **teaspoons vanilla extract**
- 1 **cup all-purpose flour**
- ½ **cup HERSHEY'S Cocoa**
- ½ **teaspoon baking soda**
- ½ **teaspoon salt**
- 2 **cups (12-ounce package) HERSHEY'S SPECIAL DARK® Chocolate Chips**
- 1 **cup chopped nuts**
  **Powdered sugar (optional)**

**1.** Heat oven to 350°F.

**2.** Beat butter and shortening with electric mixer on medium speed in large bowl until well blended. Add brown sugar and granulated sugar; beat thoroughly. Add egg, milk and vanilla, beating until well blended.

**3.** Stir together flour, cocoa, baking soda and salt; gradually beat into butter mixture. Stir in chocolate chips and nuts. Drop by teaspoons onto ungreased cookie sheet.

**4.** Bake 10 to 12 minutes or until edges are set. Cool slightly. Remove to wire rack and cool completely. Sprinkle with powdered sugar, if desired.

# KISSES® BRAND

## Fluted KISSES® Cups with Peanut Butter Filling

*Makes about 2 dozen pieces*

> **72 HERSHEY¡S KISSES®BRAND Milk Chocolates, divided**
> **1 cup REESE'S® Creamy Peanut Butter**
> **1 cup powdered sugar**
> **1 tablespoon butter or margarine, softened**

**1.** Line small baking cups (1¾ inches in diameter) with small paper baking liners. Remove wrappers from chocolates.

**2.** Place 48 chocolates in small microwave-safe bowl. Microwave on HIGH (100%) 1 minute or until chocolate is melted and smooth when stirred. Using small brush, coat inside of paper cups with melted chocolate.

**3.** Refrigerate 20 minutes; reapply melted chocolate to any thin spots. Refrigerate until firm, preferably overnight. Gently peel paper from chocolate cups.

**4.** Beat peanut butter, powdered sugar and butter with electric mixer on medium speed in small bowl until smooth. Spoon into chocolate cups. Before serving, top each cup with a chocolate piece. Cover; store cups in refrigerator.

Fluted KISSES® Cups with Peanut Butter Filling

# HERSHEY'S Triple Chocolate Cookies

*Makes about 4 dozen cookies*

48 **HERSHEY'S KISSES®**BRAND **Milk Chocolates or HERSHEY'S KISSES®**BRAND **WITH ALMONDS Chocolates**
½ **cup (1 stick) butter or margarine, softened**
¾ **cup granulated sugar**
¾ **cup packed light brown sugar**
1 **teaspoon vanilla extract**
2 **eggs**
1 **tablespoon milk**
2¼ **cups all-purpose flour**
⅓ **cup HERSHEY'S Cocoa**
1 **teaspoon baking soda**
½ **teaspoon salt**
1 **cup HERSHEY'S Semi-Sweet Chocolate Chips**

**1.** Remove wrappers from chocolates. Heat oven to 350°F.

**2.** Beat butter, granulated sugar, brown sugar and vanilla with electric mixer on medium speed in large bowl until well blended. Add eggs and milk; beat well.

**3.** Stir together flour, cocoa, baking soda and salt; gradually beat into butter mixture, beating until well blended. Stir in chocolate chips. Shape dough into 1-inch balls. Place on ungreased cookie sheet.

**4.** Bake 10 to 11 minutes or until set. Gently press a chocolate into center of each cookie. Remove to wire rack and cool completely.

**VARIATION:** For vanilla cookies, omit cocoa and add an additional ⅓ cup all-purpose flour.

# Secret KISSES® Cookies

*Makes 3 dozen cookies*

- **1 cup (2 sticks) butter or margarine, softened**
- **½ cup granulated sugar**
- **1 teaspoon vanilla extract**
- **1¾ cups all-purpose flour**
- **1 cup finely chopped walnuts or almonds**
- **36 HERSHEY'S KISSES®BRAND Milk Chocolates or HERSHEY'S KISSES®BRAND WITH ALMONDS Chocolates**
- **Powdered sugar**

**1.** Beat butter, granulated sugar and vanilla with electric mixer on medium speed in large bowl until fluffy. Add flour and walnuts; mix on low speed until well blended. Cover; refrigerate 1 to 2 hours or until dough is firm enough to handle.

**2.** Remove wrappers from chocolates. Heat oven to 375°F. Using about 1 tablespoon dough for each cookie, shape dough around each chocolate; shape into balls. (Be sure to cover each chocolate piece completely.) Place on ungreased cookie sheets.

**3.** Bake 10 to 12 minutes or until cookies are set but not browned. Cool slightly; remove to wire rack. While still slightly warm, roll in powdered sugar. Cool completely. Store in tightly covered container. Roll again in powdered sugar just before serving.

**VARIATION:** Sift together 1 tablespoon HERSHEY'S Cocoa with ⅓ cup powdered sugar. After removing cookies from oven roll in cocoa mixture instead of powdered sugar.

## Chocolate KISSES® Mousse

*Males 4 servings*

- **36 HERSHEY'S KISSES®BRAND Milk Chocolates**
- **1½ cups miniature marshmallows or 15 regular marshmallows**
- **⅓ cup milk**
- **2 teaspoons kirsch (cherry brandy) or ¼ teaspoon almond extract**
- **6 to 8 drops red food color (optional)**
- **1 cup cold whipping cream**
  **Additional HERSHEY'S KISSES®BRAND Milk chocolates (optional)**

**1.** Remove wrappers from chocolates. Combine marshmallows and milk in small saucepan. Cook over low heat, stirring constantly, until marshmallows are melted and mixture is smooth. Remove from heat.

**2.** Pour ⅓ cup marshmallow mixture into medium bowl; stir in brandy and food color, if desired. Set aside. To remaining marshmallow mixture, add 36 chocolates; return to low heat, stirring constantly until chocolate is melted. Remove from heat; cool to room temperature.

**3.** Beat whipping cream with electric mixer on high speed in large bowl until stiff peaks form. Fold 1 cup whipped cream into chocolate mixture. Gradually fold remaining whipped cream into reserved marshmallow mixture. Fill 4 parfait glasses about ¾ full with chocolate mousse. Refrigerate chocolate mousse and whipped cream mixture 3 to 4 hours or until mousse is set. Serve mousse with whipped cream mixture; garnish with additional chocolates, if desired.

Chocolate KISSES® Mousse

# Macaroon KISSES® Cookies

*Makes about 4 dozen cookies*

- ⅓ cup butter or margarine, softened
- 1 package (3 ounces) cream cheese, softened
- ¾ cup sugar
- 1 egg yolk
- 2 teaspoons almond extract
- 2 teaspoons orange juice
- 1¼ cups all-purpose flour
- 2 teaspoons baking powder
- ¼ teaspoon salt
- 5 cups MOUNDS® Sweetened Coconut Flakes, divided
- 48 HERSHEY'S KISSES®BRAND Milk Chocolates

**1.** Beat butter, cream cheese and sugar with electric mixer on medium speed in large bowl until well blended. Add egg yolk, almond extract and orange juice; beat well. Stir together flour, baking powder and salt; gradually add to butter mixture. Stir in 3 cups coconut. Cover; refrigerate 1 hour or until firm enough to handle. Meanwhile, remove wrappers from chocolates.

**2.** Heat oven to 350°F. Shape dough into 1-inch balls; roll in remaining 2 cups coconut. Place on ungreased cookie sheet.

**3.** Bake 10 to 12 minutes or until lightly browned. Immediately press chocolate piece into center of each cookie. Cool 1 minute. Carefully remove to wire rack and cool completely.

# Chocolate Chip KISSES® Cookies

*Makes 4 dozen cookies*

- 48 HERSHEY'S KISSES®BRAND Milk Chocolates or HERSHEY'S KISSES®BRAND WITH ALMONDS Chocolates
- 1 cup (2 sticks) butter or margarine, softened
- ⅓ cup granulated sugar
- ⅓ cup packed light brown sugar
- 1 teaspoon vanilla extract
- 2 cups all-purpose flour
- 1¼ cups HERSHEY'S MINI CHIPS™ Semi-Sweet Chocolate Chips, divided
- 1 teaspoon shortening (do not use butter, margarine, spread or oil)

1. Heat oven to 375°F. Remove wrappers from chocolates.

2. Beat butter, granulated sugar, brown sugar and vanilla with electric mixer on medium speed in large bowl until well blended. Add flour to butter mixture; beat until smooth. Stir in 1 cup mini chocolate chips. Mold scant tablespoon dough around each milk chocolate piece, covering chocolates completely. Shape into balls; place 2 inches apart on ungreased cookie sheet.

3. Bake 10 to 12 minutes or until set. Cool slightly. Remove to wire rack and cool completely. Place remaining ¼ cup mini chocolate chips and shortening in small microwave-safe bowl. Microwave on HIGH (100%) 30 seconds or until chips are melted and mixture is smooth when stirred; drizzle over cookies.

35

## Peanut Blossoms

*Makes about 4 dozen cookies*

- **48 HERSHEY'S KISSES®BRAND Milk Chocolates**
- **¾ cup REESE'S® Creamy or Crunchy Peanut Butter**
- **½ cup shortening**
- **⅓ cup granulated sugar**
- **⅓ cup packed light brown sugar**
- **1 egg**
- **2 tablespoons milk**
- **1 teaspoon vanilla extract**
- **1½ cups all-purpose flour**
- **1 teaspoon baking soda**
- **½ teaspoon salt**
- **Granulated sugar**

**1.** Heat oven to 375°F. Remove wrappers from chocolates.

**2.** Beat peanut butter and shortening with electric mixer on medium speed in large bowl until well blended. Add ⅓ cup granulated sugar and brown sugar; beat until fluffy. Add egg, milk and vanilla; beat well. Stir together flour, baking soda and salt; gradually beat into peanut butter mixture.

**3.** Shape dough into 1-inch balls. Roll in additional granulated sugar; place on ungreased cookie sheet.

**4.** Bake 8 to 10 minutes or until lightly browned. Immediately press a chocolate into center of each cookie; cookie will crack around edges. Remove to wire rack and cool completely.

Peanut Blossoms

# HERSHEY'S KISSES® Birthday Cake

*Makes 10 to 12 servings*

- 2 cups sugar
- 1¾ cups all-purpose flour
- ¾ cup HERSHEY'S Cocoa or HERSHEY'S Dutch Processed Cocoa
- 1½ teaspoons baking powder
- 1½ teaspoons baking soda
- 1 teaspoon salt
- 2 eggs
- 1 cup milk
- ½ cup vegetable oil
- 2 teaspoons vanilla extract
- 1 cup boiling water
  Vanilla Buttercream Frosting (recipe follows)
  HERSHEY'S KISSES® BRAND Milk Chocolates

**1.** Heat oven to 350°F. Grease and flour two 9-inch round baking pans or one 13×9×2-inch baking pan.

**2.** Stir together sugar, flour, cocoa, baking powder, baking soda and salt in large bowl. Add eggs, milk, oil and vanilla; beat with electric mixer on medium speed for 2 minutes. Stir in boiling water (batter will be thin). Pour batter into prepared pans.

**3.** Bake 30 to 35 minutes for round pans, 35 to 40 minutes for rectangular pan or until wooden pick inserted in center comes out clean. Cool 10 minutes; turn out onto wire racks. Cool completely.

**4.** Frost with Vanilla Buttercream Frosting. Remove wrappers from chocolates. Garnish top and sides of cake with chocolates.

## Vanilla Buttercream Frosting

*Makes about 2⅓ cups frosting*

- ⅓ cup butter or margarine, softened
- 4 cups powdered sugar, divided
- 3 to 4 tablespoons milk
- 1½ teaspoons vanilla extract

Beat butter with electric mixer on medium speed in large bowl until creamy. With mixer running, gradually add about 2 cups powdered sugar, beating until well blended. Slowly beat in milk and vanilla. Gradually add remaining powdered sugar, beating until smooth. Add additional milk, if necessary, until frosting is desired consistency.

HERSHEY'S KISSES® Birthday Cake

# Christmas KISSES® Candies

*Makes about 14 candies*

**About 14 HERSHEY'S KISSES®BRAND Milk Chocolates**
¾ **cup ground almonds**
⅓ **cup powdered sugar**
1 **tablespoon light corn syrup**
½ **teaspoon almond extract**
**Few drops green food color**
**Few drops red food color**
**Granulated sugar**

**1.** Remove wrappers from chocolates. Stir together ground almonds and powdered sugar in medium bowl until well blended. Stir together corn syrup and almond extract; pour over almond mixture, stirring until completely blended. Divide mixture between two bowls.

**2.** Stir green food color into one bowl; with clean hands, mix until color is well blended and mixture clings together. Repeat with red food color and remaining ground almond mixture.

**3.** Shape at least 1 teaspoon colored almond mixture around each chocolate. Roll in granulated sugar.

## HUGS® & KISSES® Crescents

*Makes 8 crescents*

> 1 package (8 ounces) refrigerated crescent dinner rolls
> 24 HERSHEY'S KISSES®BRAND Milk Chocolates or HERSHEY'S HUGS® Chocolates
> Powdered sugar

**1.** Heat oven to 375°F. Separate dough into 8 triangles. Remove wrappers from chocolates.

**2.** Place 3 chocolates at center of wide end of each triangle; chocolates on each piece of dough should be touching one another. Starting at wide end, roll to opposite point; pinch edges to seal. Place rolls, pointed side down, on ungreased cookie sheet. Curve into crescent shape.

**3.** Bake 10 minutes or until lightly browned. Cool slightly; sprinkle with powdered sugar. Serve warm.

NOTE: Leftover crescents can be reheated in microwave for a few seconds.

## Candy-Kissed Twists

*Makes about 36 pieces*

> HERSHEY'S KISSES®BRAND Milk Chocolates
> 1 bag small pretzels (twisted)
> Decorative garnishes such as: REESE'S® PIECES® Candies, silver dragées, small holiday themed candies, nut pieces, miniature marshmallows, candied cherry pieces

**1.** Heat oven to 350°F. Remove wrappers from chocolates.

**2.** Place pretzels on ungreased cookie sheet. Place a chocolate on top of each pretzel.

**3.** Bake 2 to 3 minutes or until the chocolate is soft, but not melting.

**4.** Remove from oven; gently press decorative garnish on top of softened chocolate piece. Cool.

## REESE'S® Peanut Butter & HERSHEY'S KISSES® Pie

*Makes 8 servings*

**About 42 HERSHEY'S KISSES®BRAND Milk Chocolates, divided**
2 **tablespoons milk**
1 **packaged (8-inch) crumb crust (6 ounces)**
1 **package (8 ounces) cream cheese, softened**
¾ **cup sugar**
1 **cup REESE'S® Creamy or Crunchy Peanut Butter**
1 **tub (8 ounces) frozen non-dairy whipped topping, thawed and divided**

**1.** Remove wrappers from chocolates. Place 26 chocolates and milk in small microwave-safe bowl. Microwave on HIGH (100%) 1 minute or just until melted and smooth when stirred. Spread evenly on bottom of crust. Refrigerate about 30 minutes.

**2.** Beat cream cheese with electric mixer on medium speed in medium bowl until smooth; gradually beat in sugar, then peanut butter, beating well after each addition. Reserve ½ cup whipped topping; fold remaining whipped topping into peanut butter mixture. Spoon into crust over chocolate. Cover; refrigerate about 6 hours or until set.

**3.** Garnish with reserved whipped topping and remaining chocolates. Cover; refrigerate leftover pie.

REESE'S® Peanut Butter & HERSHEY'S KISSES® Pie

# Chocolate Lover's Ice Cream Sauce

*Makes about 1 cup sauce*

**30 HERSHEY'S KISSES®ʙʀᴀɴᴅ Milk Chocolates**
**½ cup HERSHEY'S Syrup**
**Any flavor ice cream**
**Sweetened whipped cream**
**Additional HERSHEY'S KISSES®ʙʀᴀɴᴅ Milk Chocolates**
**(optional)**

**1.** Remove wrappers from chocolates.

**2.** Combine chocolates and syrup in small heavy saucepan. Stir constantly over very low heat until chocolates are melted and mixture is smooth when stirred; remove from heat.

**3.** Spoon sauce over scoops of ice cream. Garnish with sweetened whipped cream and additional chocolates, if desired. Serve immediately. Cover and refrigerate leftover sauce.

**TO REHEAT:** Place smaller bowl containing sauce in large bowl containing about 1 inch very hot water. Allow to stand several minutes to soften; stir to desired consistency.

**MICROWAVE DIRECTIONS:** Combine chocolates and syrup in small microwave-safe bowl. Microwave on HIGH (100%) 15 seconds; stir well. Microwave an additional 30 seconds; stir until chocolates are melted and mixture is smooth when stirred. If necessary, microwave an additional 15 seconds or as needed to melt chocolates. To reheat refrigerated sauce, microwave on HIGH a few seconds at a time; stir. Repeat until warm.

## Sweetheart KISSES® Cookies

*Yield will vary according to cookie recipe used*

**Sugar Cookie Dough (purchased or your favorite recipe)**
**HERSHEY₅S Cocoa**
48 **HERSHEY₅S KISSES®**BRAND **Milk Chocolates, unwrapped***
1 **teaspoon shortening (do not use butter, margarine, spread**
**or oil)**

*\*Forty-eight KISSES®*BRAND *Milk Chocolates is enough to garnish about 3 dozen cookies following these directions, adjust as necessary for sugar cookie recipe.*

**1.** Heat oven to as directed for sugar cookies. Divide dough in half; roll out one half at a time to ¼-inch thickness following package or recipe directions. Cut out with 2-inch heart shaped cookie cutters; place on ungreased cookie sheet.

**2.** Bake according to package or recipe directions. Cool completely on cooling racks. Sprinkle cookie with cocoa.

**3.** Place 12 chocolates and shortening in small microwave-safe bowl. Microwave on HIGH (100%) 1 minute or until chocolates are melted and mixture is smooth when stirred. Drizzle over cookies. Before drizzle sets, place 1 chocolate in center of each heart.

# cakes &
# cheesecakes

## HERSHEY'S Chocolate Peppermint Roll

*Makes 10 to 12 servings*

**CHOCOLATE SPONGE ROLL**

- 4 eggs, separated
- ½ cup plus ⅓ cup granulated sugar, divided
- 1 teaspoon vanilla extract
- ½ cup all-purpose flour
- ⅓ cup HERSHEY'S Cocoa
- ½ teaspoon baking powder
- ¼ teaspoon baking soda
- ⅛ teaspoon salt
- ⅓ cup water

**PEPPERMINT FILLING**

- 1 cup whipping cream, cold
- ¼ cup powdered sugar
- ¼ cup finely crushed hard peppermint candy or ½ teaspoon mint extract
- Few drops red food color (optional)

**CHOCOLATE GLAZE**

- 2 tablespoons butter or margarine
- 2 tablespoons HERSHEY'S Cocoa
- 2 tablespoons water
- 1 cup powdered sugar
- ½ teaspoon vanilla extract

*continued on page 48*

HERSHEY'S Chocolate Peppermint Roll

*HERSHEY'S Chocolate Peppermint Roll, continued*

**1.** For Chocolate Sponge Roll, heat oven to 375°F. Line 15½×10½×1-inch jelly-roll pan with foil; generously grease foil.

**2.** Beat egg whites with electric mixer on high speed in large bowl until soft peaks form; gradually add ½ cup granulated sugar, beating until stiff peaks form. Set aside.

**3.** Beat egg yolks and vanilla with electric mixer on medium speed in medium bowl 3 minutes. Gradually add remaining ⅓ cup granulated sugar; continue beating 2 minutes. Stir together flour, cocoa, baking powder, baking soda and salt. With mixer on low speed, add flour mixture to egg yolk mixture alternately with water, beating just until batter is smooth. Using rubber spatula, gradually fold beaten egg whites into chocolate mixture until well blended. Spread batter evenly in prepared pan.

**4.** Bake 12 to 15 minutes or until top springs back when touched lightly. Immediately loosen cake from edges of pan; invert onto clean towel sprinkled with powdered sugar. Carefully peel off foil. Immediately roll cake in towel, starting from narrow end; place on wire rack to cool completely.

**5.** For Peppermint Filling, beat whipping cream with electric mixer on medium speed in medium bowl until slightly thickened. Add ¼ cup powdered sugar and peppermint candy or mint extract and food color, if desired; beat cream until stiff peaks form.

**6.** For Chocolate Glaze, melt butter in small saucepan over very low heat; add cocoa and water, stirring until smooth and slightly thickened. Remove from heat and cool slightly. (Cool completely for thicker frosting.) Gradually beat in 1 cup powdered sugar and vanilla extract.

**7.** Carefully unroll cake; remove towel. Spread cake with Peppermint Filling; reroll cake. Glaze with Chocolate Glaze. Refrigerate until just before serving. Cover; refrigerate leftover dessert.

**VARIATION:** Substitute Coffee Filling for Peppermint Filling. Combine 1½ cups cold milk and 2 teaspoons instant coffee granules in medium bowl; let stand 5 minutes. Add 1 package (4-serving size) instant vanilla pudding. Beat with electric mixer on lowest speed about 2 minutes or until well blended. Use as directed above to fill Chocolate Sponge Roll.

## Chocolate Syrup Swirl Cake

*Makes 20 servings*

1 cup (2 sticks) butter or margarine, softened
2 cups sugar
2 teaspoons vanilla extract
3 eggs
2¾ cups all-purpose flour
1¼ teaspoons baking soda, divided
½ teaspoon salt
1 cup buttermilk or sour milk*
1 cup HERSHEY'S Syrup
1 cup MOUNDS® Sweetened Coconut Flakes (optional)

*To sour milk: Use 1 tablespoon white vinegar plus milk to equal 1 cup.*

**1.** Heat oven to 350°F. Grease and flour 12-cup fluted tube pan or 10-inch tube pan.

**2.** Beat butter, sugar and vanilla in large bowl until fluffy. Add eggs; beat until well blended. Stir together flour, 1 teaspoon baking soda and salt; add alternately with buttermilk to butter mixture, beating until well blended.

**3.** Measure 2 cups batter in small bowl; stir in syrup and remaining ¼ teaspoon baking soda. Add coconut, if desired, to remaining vanilla batter; pour into prepared pan. Pour chocolate batter over vanilla batter in pan; do not mix.

**4.** Bake 60 to 70 minutes or until wooden pick inserted in center comes out clean. Cool 15 minutes; remove from pan to wire rack. Cool completely on wire rack; glaze or frost as desired.

## Holiday Coconut Cake
*Makes 12 servings*

**COCONUT CAKE**
- ½ cup (1 stick) butter or margarine, softened
- ½ cup shortening
- 2 cups sugar
- 5 eggs, separated
- 1 teaspoon vanilla extract
- 2 cups all-purpose flour
- 1 teaspoon baking soda
- ¼ teaspoon salt
- 1 cup buttermilk
- 2 cups MOUNDS® Sweetened Coconut Flakes
- ½ cup chopped pecans

**TOFFEE CREAM**
- 2 cups cold whipping cream
- ¼ cup powdered sugar
- 1 teaspoon vanilla extract
- ½ cup HEATH® BITS 'O BRICKLE® Toffee Bits
- Additional HEATH® BITS 'O BRICKLE® Toffee Bits (optional)

**1.** Heat oven to 350°F. Grease and flour 12-cup fluted tube pan.

**2.** Beat butter, shortening, sugar, egg yolks and vanilla with electric mixer on medium speed in large bowl until creamy. Stir together flour, baking soda and salt; add alternately with buttermilk, beating until well blended. Stir in coconut and pecans.

**3.** Beat egg whites with electric mixer on high speed in large bowl until stiff peaks form; fold into batter. Pour batter into prepared pan.

**4.** Bake 45 to 55 minutes or until wooden pick inserted in center comes out clean. Cool 10 minutes; remove from pan to wire rack. Cool completely.

**5.** For Toffee Cream, beat whipping cream, powdered sugar and vanilla with electric mixer on medium speed in large bowl until stiff peaks form. Fold in toffee bits. Frost cake with Toffee Cream. Garnish with additional toffee bits, if desired. Cover; store leftover cake in refrigerator.

Holiday Coconut Cake

## HERSHEY'S SPECIAL DARK® Truffle Brownie Cheesecake

*Makes 10 to 12 servings*

**BROWNIE LAYER**

- 6 tablespoons melted butter or margarine
- 1¼ cups sugar
- 1 teaspoon vanilla extract
- 2 eggs
- 1 cup plus 2 tablespoons all-purpose flour
- ⅓ cup HERSHEY'S Cocoa
- ½ teaspoon *each* baking powder and salt

**TRUFFLE CHEESECAKE LAYER**

- 3 packages (8 ounces each) cream cheese, softened
- ¾ cup sugar
- 4 eggs
- ¼ cup heavy cream
- 2 teaspoons vanilla extract
- ¼ teaspoon salt
- 2 cups (12-ounce package) HERSHEY'S SPECIAL DARK® Chocolate Chips, divided
- ½ teaspoon shortening (do not use butter, margarine, spread or oil)

**1.** Heat oven to 350°F. Grease 9-inch springform pan.

**2.** For Brownie Layer, stir together melted butter, 1¼ cups sugar and 1 teaspoon vanilla. Add 2 eggs; stir until blended. Stir in flour, cocoa, baking powder and ½ teaspoon salt; blend well. Spread in prepared pan. Bake 25 to 30 minutes or until brownie layer pulls away from sides of pan.

**3.** Meanwhile for Truffle Cheesecake Layer, beat cream cheese and ¾ cup sugar in large bowl until smooth. Gradually beat in 4 eggs, heavy cream, 2 teaspoons vanilla and ¼ teaspoon salt until blended.

**4.** Set aside 2 tablespoons chocolate chips. Place remaining chips in large microwave-safe bowl. Microwave on HIGH (100%) 1½ minutes or until smooth when stirred. Blend melted chocolate into cheesecake batter.

**5.** Remove Brownie Layer from oven and immediately spoon cheesecake mixture over brownie. Return to oven; continue baking 45 to 50 minutes or until center is almost set. Remove from oven to wire rack. With knife, loosen cake from side of pan. Cool to room temperature. Remove side of pan.

**6.** Place remaining 2 tablespoons chocolate chips and shortening in small microwave-safe bowl. Microwave on HIGH (100%) 30 seconds or until smooth when stirred. Drizzle over top of cheesecake. Cover; refrigerate several hours. Cover and refrigerate leftover cheesecake.

HERSHEY'S SPECIAL DARK® Truffle Brownie Cheesecake

## Cinnamon Chip Applesauce Coffeecake

*Makes 12 to 15 servings*

- **1 cup (2 sticks) butter or margarine, softened**
- **1 cup granulated sugar**
- **2 eggs**
- **½ teaspoon vanilla extract**
- **¾ cup applesauce**
- **2½ cups all-purpose flour**
- **1 teaspoon baking soda**
- **½ teaspoon salt**
- **1⅔ cups (10-ounce package) HERSHEY'S Cinnamon Chips**
- **1 cup chopped pecans (optional)**
- **¾ cup powdered sugar**
- **1 to 2 tablespoons warm water**

**1.** Heat oven to 350°F. Lightly grease 13×9×2-inch baking pan.

**2.** Beat butter and sugar with electric mixer on medium speed in large bowl until well blended. Beat in eggs and vanilla. Mix in applesauce. Stir together flour, baking soda and salt; gradually add to butter mixture, beating until well blended. Stir in cinnamon chips and pecans, if desired. Spread in prepared pan.

**3.** Bake 30 to 35 minutes or until wooden pick inserted in center comes out clean. Cool in pan on wire rack. Stir together powdered sugar and warm water to make smooth glaze; drizzle cake with glaze or sprinkle with powdered sugar, as desired. Serve at room temperature or while still slightly warm.

**FLUTED CAKE:** Grease and flour 12-cup fluted tube pan. Prepare batter as directed; pour into prepared pan. Bake 45 to 50 minutes or until wooden pick inserted in thickest part comes out clean. Cool 15 minutes; invert onto wire rack. Cool completely.

**CUPCAKES:** Line 24 baking cups (2½-inches in diameter) with paper baking liners. Prepare batter as directed; divide evenly into prepared cups. Bake 15 to 18 minutes or until wooden pick inserted in center comes out clean. Cool completely.

Cinnamon Chip Applesauce Coffeecake

## Chilled Raspberry Cheesecake

*Makes 10 to 12 servings*

**CRUST**

- 1½ cups (about 45 wafers) vanilla wafer crumbs
- ⅓ cup HERSHEY'S Cocoa
- ⅓ cup powdered sugar
- ⅓ cup butter or margarine, melted
- 3 tablespoons seedless red raspberry preserves

**CHEESECAKE**

- 1 package (10 ounces) frozen raspberries, thawed
- 1 envelope unflavored gelatin
- ½ cup cold water
- ½ cup boiling water
- 2 packages (8 ounces each) cream cheese, softened
- ½ cup granulated sugar
- 1 teaspoon vanilla extract

**CHOCOLATE WHIPPED CREAM**

- ½ cup powdered sugar
- ¼ cup HERSHEY'S Cocoa
- 1 cup cold whipping cream
- 1 teaspoon vanilla extract
- Fresh raspberries
- Mint leaves (optional)

1. Heat oven to 350°F.

2. For Crust, stir together crumbs, ⅓ cup cocoa and ⅓ cup powdered sugar in medium bowl; stir in melted butter. Press mixture onto bottom and 1½ inches up side of 9-inch springform pan. Bake 10 minutes; cool completely. Spread raspberry preserves over cooled crust.

3. For Cheesecake, purée and strain raspberries; set aside. Sprinkle gelatin over cold water in small bowl; let stand several minutes to soften. Add boiling water; stir until gelatin dissolves completely and mixture is clear. Beat cream cheese, granulated sugar and 1 teaspoon vanilla in large bowl until smooth. Gradually add raspberry purée and gelatin, mixing thoroughly; pour into prepared crust. Refrigerate several hours or overnight. Loosen cake from side of pan with knife; remove side of pan.

4. For Chocolate Whipped Cream, combine ½ cup powdered sugar and ¼ cup cocoa in medium bowl. Add whipping cream and 1 teaspoon vanilla; beat until stiff peaks form. Garnish cheesecake with chocolate whipped cream, raspberries and mint, if desired. Cover; refrigerate leftover cheesecake.

Chilled Raspberry Cheesecake

# Trimmed Down Chocoberry Cheesecake

*Makes 14 servings*

**GRAHAM CRUST**
- ½ cup graham cracker crumbs
- 1 tablespoon melted margarine

**CHOCOBERRY CHEESECAKE**
- 1 container (8 ounces) nonfat cottage cheese
- 1 package (8 ounces) Neufchâtel cheese (⅓ less fat cream cheese), softened
- 1 cup sugar*
- ⅓ cup HERSHEY'S Dutch Processed Cocoa or HERSHEY'S Cocoa
- 1 package (10 ounces) frozen strawberries in syrup, thawed and drained
- ⅓ cup liquid egg substitute
- Frozen light non-dairy whipped topping, thawed (optional)
- Additional strawberries (optional)

*To reduce calories, replace sugar with 1 cup sucralose sugar substitute.*

**1.** For Graham Crust, stir together graham cracker crumbs and melted margarine in small bowl; press onto bottom of 8-inch springform pan.

**2.** For Chocoberry Cheesecake, heat oven to 325°F. Place cottage cheese in food processor; process until smooth. Add Neufchâtel cheese, sugar, cocoa and strawberries; process until smooth. Stir in egg substitute. Pour gently over prepared crust.

**3.** Bake 55 to 60 minutes or just until almost set in center. With knife, loosen cheesecake from side of pan. Cool completely in pan on wire rack. Cover; refrigerate until chilled. Just before serving, remove side of pan. Serve with whipped topping and additional strawberries, if desired. Cover; refrigerate leftover cheesecake.

Trimmed Down Chocoberry Cheesecake

# brownies &
# bars

## Chocolate-Almond Honeys

*Makes 20 bars*

- 1¾ cups graham cracker crumbs
- 1 can (14 ounces) sweetened condensed milk (not evaporated milk)
- 2 tablespoons honey
- 2 tablespoons orange or apple juice
- 1 teaspoon freshly grated orange peel
- 1 cup HERSHEY'S Semi-Sweet Chocolate Chips
- ½ cup chopped blanched almonds

**1.** Heat oven to 350°F. Grease 9-inch square baking pan.

**2.** Stir together graham cracker crumbs, sweetened condensed milk, honey, orange juice and orange peel in large bowl. Stir in chocolate chips and almonds. Spread batter in prepared pan.

**3.** Bake 30 minutes or until golden brown. Cool completely in pan on wire rack. Cut into bars.

Chocolate-Almond Honeys

# Chewy Toffee Almond Bars
*Makes 36 bars*

> 1 **cup (2 sticks) butter, softened**
> ½ **cup sugar**
> 2 **cups all-purpose flour**
> 1⅓ **cups (8-ounce package) HEATH® BITS 'O BRICKLE®**
> **Almond Toffee Bits**
> ¾ **cup light corn syrup**
> 1 **cup sliced almonds, divided**
> ¾ **cup MOUNDS® Sweetened Coconut Flakes, divided**

**1.** Heat oven to 350°F. Grease sides of 13×9×2-inch baking pan.

**2.** Beat butter and sugar with electric mixer on medium speed in large bowl until fluffy. Gradually add flour, beating until well blended. Press dough evenly into prepared pan. Bake 15 to 20 minutes or until edges are lightly browned.

**3.** Meanwhile, combine toffee bits and corn syrup in medium saucepan. Cook over medium heat, stirring constantly, until toffee is melted (about 10 to 12 minutes). Stir in ½ cup almonds and ½ cup coconut. Spread toffee mixture to within ¼ inch of edges of crust. Sprinkle remaining ½ cup almonds and remaining ¼ cup coconut over top.

**4.** Bake an additional 15 minutes or until bubbly. Cool completely in pan on wire rack. Cut into bars.

Chewy Toffee Almond Bars

# Chocolate Orange Cheesecake Bars

*Makes 24 bars*

**CRUST**
- 1 **cup all-purpose flour**
- ½ **cup packed light brown sugar**
- ¼ **teaspoon ground cinnamon (optional)**
- ⅓ **cup shortening**
- ½ **cup chopped pecans**

**CHOCOLATE ORANGE FILLING**
- 1 **package (8 ounces) cream cheese, softened**
- ⅔ **cup granulated sugar**
- ⅓ **cup HERSHEY'S Cocoa**
- ¼ **cup milk**
- 1 **egg**
- 1 **teaspoon vanilla extract**
- ¼ **teaspoon freshly grated orange peel**
  **Pecan halves (optional)**

**1.** Heat oven to 350°F.

**2.** For Crust, stir together flour, brown sugar and cinnamon, if desired, in large bowl. Cut shortening into flour mixture with pastry blender or two knives until mixture resembles coarse crumbs. Stir in chopped pecans. Reserve ¾ cup flour mixture. Press remaining mixture firmly onto bottom of ungreased 9-inch square baking pan. Bake 10 minutes or until lightly browned.

**3.** For Chocolate Orange Filling, beat cream cheese and sugar with electric mixer on medium speed in medium bowl until fluffy. Add cocoa, milk, egg, vanilla and orange peel; beat until smooth.

**4.** Spread filling over warm crust. Sprinkle with reserved flour mixture. Press pecan halves lightly onto top, if desired. Return to oven. Bake 25 to 30 minutes or until lightly browned. Cool; cut into bars. Cover; refrigerate leftover bars.

Chocolate Orange Cheesecake Bars

# White Chip Lemon Streusel Bars

*Makes 36 bars*

> 1 can (14 ounces) sweetened condensed milk (not evaporated milk)
> ½ cup lemon juice
> 1 teaspoon freshly grated lemon peel
> 2 cups (12-ounce package) HERSHEY'S Premier White Chips, divided
> ⅔ cup butter or margarine, softened
> 1 cup packed light brown sugar
> 1½ cups all-purpose flour
> 1½ cups regular rolled or quick-cooking oats
> ¾ cup toasted pecan pieces*
> 1 teaspoon baking powder
> ½ teaspoon salt
> 1 egg
> ½ teaspoon shortening

*\*To toast pecans: Heat oven to 350°F. Spread pecans in thin layer in shallow baking pan. Bake, stirring occasionally, 7 to 8 minutes or until golden brown; cool.*

**1.** Heat oven to 350°F. Lightly grease 13×9×2-inch baking pan. Combine sweetened condensed milk, lemon juice and lemon peel in medium bowl; set aside. Measure out ¼ cup and ⅓ cup white chips; set aside. Add remaining white chips to lemon mixture.

**2.** Beat butter and brown sugar with electric mixer on medium speed in large bowl until well blended. Stir together flour, oats, pecans, baking powder and salt; add to butter mixture, blending well. Set aside 1⅔ cups oats mixture. Add egg to remaining oats mixture, blending until crumbly; press onto bottom of prepared pan. Gently spoon lemon mixture on top, spreading evenly. Add reserved ⅓ cup white chips to reserved oats mixture. Sprinkle over lemon layer, pressing down lightly.

**3.** Bake 20 to 25 minutes or until lightly browned. Cool in pan on wire rack. Place remaining ¼ cup white chips and shortening in small microwave-safe bowl. Microwave at HIGH (100%) 30 seconds or until chips are melted and mixture is smooth when stirred. Drizzle over baked bars. Allow drizzle to set; cut into bars.

White Chip Lemon Streusel Bars

## Peanut Butter Fudge Brownie Bars

*Makes 36 bars*

> 1 cup (2 sticks) butter or margarine, melted
> 1½ cups sugar
> 2 eggs
> 1 teaspoon vanilla extract
> 1¼ cups all-purpose flour
> ⅔ cup HERSHEY'S Cocoa
> ¼ cup milk
> 1¼ cups chopped pecans or walnuts, divided
> ½ cup (1 stick) butter or margarine
> 1⅔ cups (10-ounce package) REESE'S® Peanut Butter Chips
> 1 can (14 ounces) sweetened condensed milk (not evaporated milk)
> ¼ cup HERSHEY'S Semi-Sweet Chocolate Chips

**1.** Heat oven to 350°F. Grease 13×9×2-inch baking pan.

**2.** Beat melted butter, sugar, eggs and vanilla with electric mixer on medium speed in large bowl until well blended. Add flour, cocoa and milk; beat until blended. Stir in 1 cup nuts. Spread in prepared pan.

**3.** Bake 25 to 30 minutes or just until edges begin to pull away from sides of pan. Cool completely in pan on wire rack.

**4.** Melt ½ cup butter and peanut butter chips in medium saucepan over low heat, stirring constantly. Add sweetened condensed milk; stirring until smooth; pour over baked layer.

**5.** Place chocolate chips in small microwave-safe bowl. Microwave at HIGH (100%) 45 seconds or just until chips are melted when stirred. Drizzle bars with melted chocolate; sprinkle with remaining ¼ cup nuts. Refrigerate 1 hour or until firm. Cut into bars. Cover; refrigerate leftover bars.

Peanut Butter Fudge Brownie Bars

# Rich Chocolate Chip Toffee Bars

*Makes 48 bars*

- 2⅓ **cups all-purpose flour**
- ⅔ **cup packed light brown sugar**
- ¾ **cup (1½ sticks) butter or margarine**
- 1 **egg, lightly beaten**
- 2 **cups (12-ounce package) HERSHEY'S Semi-Sweet Chocolate Chips, divided**
- 1 **cup coarsely chopped nuts**
- 1 **can (14 ounces) sweetened condensed milk (not evaporated milk)**
- 1⅓ **cups (8-ounce package) HEATH® BITS 'O BRICKLE® Almond Toffee Bits, divided**

**1.** Heat oven to 350°F. Grease 13×9×2-inch baking pan.

**2.** Combine flour and brown sugar in large bowl. Cut butter into flour mixture with pastry blender or two knives until mixture resembles coarse crumbs. Add egg; mix well. Stir in 1½ cups chocolate chips and nuts; set aside 1½ cups mixture.

**3.** Press remaining crumb mixture onto bottom of prepared pan. Bake 10 minutes. Pour sweetened condensed milk evenly over hot crust. Set aside ¼ cup toffee bits. Sprinkle remaining toffee bits over sweetened condensed milk. Sprinkle reserved crumb mixture and remaining ½ cup chocolate chips over top.

**4.** Bake 25 to 30 minutes or until golden brown. Top with reserved ½ cup toffee bits. Cool completely in pan on wire rack. Cut into bars.

## MINI KISSES® Fruit Bars

*Makes 36 bars*

  1½  **cups all-purpose flour**
  1½  **cups quick-cooking rolled oats**
   1  **cup packed light brown sugar**
   1  **teaspoon baking powder**
  ¾  **cup (1½ sticks) butter or margarine, softened**
   1  **jar (10 to 12 ounces) raspberry jam**
  1¾  **cups (10-ounce package) HERSHEY'S MINI KISSES®BRAND Milk Chocolates**
  ½  **cup chopped nuts (optional)**

**1.** Heat oven to 350°F. Lightly grease 13×9×2-inch baking pan.

**2.** Combine flour, oats, brown sugar and baking powder in large bowl. Cut butter into flour mixture with pastry blender or two knives until mixture resembles coarse crumbs. Set aside 2 cups crumb mixture.

**3.** Press remaining crumb mixture onto bottom of prepared pan. Stir jam to soften; carefully spread over crumb mixture. Sprinkle chocolates evenly over jam. Cover with reserved crumbs. Sprinkle nuts over top, if desired; press down firmly.

**4.** Bake 40 to 45 minutes or until lightly browned. Cool completely in pan on wire rack. Cut into bars.

## Mini Brownie Cups

*Makes 24 servings*

**BROWNIE CUPS**
- 2 **egg whites**
- 1 **egg**
- ¾ **cup granulated sugar***
- ⅔ **cup all-purpose flour**
- ⅓ **cup HERSHEY'S Cocoa**
- ½ **teaspoon baking powder**
- ¼ **teaspoon salt**
- ¼ **cup (½ stick) reduced-fat margarine, melted and cooled**

**MOCHA GLAZE**
- ¼ **cup powdered sugar**
- ¾ **teaspoon HERSHEY'S Cocoa**
- ¼ **teaspoon powdered instant coffee**
- 2 **teaspoons hot water**
- ¼ **teaspoon vanilla extract**

*\*To reduce calories, replace up to half the granulated sugar with an equivalent amount of sucralose sugar substitute (sold as Splenda®). Reduce baking time by 2 to 3 minutes.*

**1.** For Brownie Cups, heat oven to 350°F. Line small muffin cups (1¾ inches in diameter) with paper baking cups or spray with vegetable cooking spray.

**2.** Beat egg whites and egg with electric mixer on medium speed in small bowl until foamy; gradually add sugar, beating until slightly thickened and light in color.

**3.** Stir together flour, cocoa, baking powder and salt; gradually add to egg mixture, beating until blended. Gradually beat in melted margarine, mixing just until blended. Fill muffin cups ⅔ full with batter. Bake 15 to 18 minutes or until wooden pick inserted in center comes out clean. Remove from pan to wire rack. Cool completely.

**4.** For Mocha Glaze, stir together powdered sugar and cocoa in small bowl. Dissolve coffee in water; gradually add to sugar mixture, stirring until well blended. Stir in vanilla.

**5.** Drizzle Brownie Cups with glaze; let stand until glaze is set. Store, covered, at room temperature.

Mini Brownie Cups

## Toffee-Topped Cheesecake Bars

*Makes 36 bars*

- 1⅓ **cups all-purpose flour**
- 1 **cup powdered sugar**
- ⅓ **cup HERSHEY'S Cocoa**
- ¼ **teaspoon baking soda**
- ¾ **cup (1½ sticks) butter or margarine, softened**
- 1 **package (8 ounces) cream cheese, softened**
- 1 **can (14 ounces) sweetened condensed milk (not evaporated milk)**
- 2 **eggs**
- 1 **teaspoon vanilla extract**
- 1⅓ **cups (8-ounce package) HEATH® BITS 'O BRICKLE® Almond Toffee Bits, divided**

**1.** Heat oven to 350°F.

**2.** Combine flour, powdered sugar, cocoa and baking soda in medium bowl; cut butter into flour mixture with pastry blender or two knives until mixture resembles coarse crumbs. Press onto bottom of ungreased 13×9×2-inch baking pan. Bake 15 minutes.

**3.** Beat cream cheese with electric mixer on medium speed in large bowl until fluffy. Add sweetened condensed milk, eggs and vanilla; beat until smooth. Stir in ¾ cup toffee bits. Pour mixture over hot crust. Bake 20 to 25 minutes or until set and edges just begin to brown. Cool 15 minutes.

**4.** Sprinkle remaining toffee bits evenly over top. Cool completely. Refrigerate several hours or until cold. Cover; store leftover bars in refrigerator.

# Fudgey SPECIAL DARK® Brownies

*Makes about 36 brownies*

  ¾ **cup HERSHEY₀S Cocoa**
  ½ **teaspoon baking soda**
  ⅔ **cup butter or margarine, melted and divided**
  ½ **cup boiling water**
  2 **cups sugar**
  2 **eggs**
1⅓ **cups all-purpose flour**
  1 **teaspoon vanilla extract**
  ¼ **teaspoon salt**
  1 **cup HERSHEY₀S SPECIAL DARK® Chocolate Chips**

**1.** Heat oven to 350°F. Grease 13×9×2-inch baking pan.

**2.** Stir together cocoa and baking soda in large bowl; stir in ⅓ cup butter. Add boiling water; stir until mixture thickens. Stir in sugar, eggs and remaining ⅓ cup butter; stir until smooth. Add flour, vanilla and salt; blend completely. Stir in chocolate chips. Pour into prepared pan.

**3.** Bake 35 to 40 minutes or until brownies begin to pull away from sides of pan. Cool completely in pan on wire rack. Frost if desired. Cut into bars.

# pies & desserts

## SPECIAL DARK® Fudge Fondue

*Makes 1½ cups fondue*

- 2 cups (12-ounce package) HERSHEY'S SPECIAL DARK® Chocolate Chips
- ½ cup light cream
- 2 teaspoons vanilla extract
  Assorted fondue dippers such as marshmallows, cherries, grapes, mandarin orange segments, pineapple chunks, strawberries, slices of other fresh fruits, small pieces of cake, or small brownies

1. Place chocolate chips and light cream in medium microwave-safe bowl. Microwave on HIGH (100%) 1 minute or just until chips are melted and mixture is smooth when stirred. Stir in vanilla.

2. Pour into fondue pot or chafing dish; serve warm with fondue dippers. If mixture thickens, stir in additional light cream, one tablespoon at a time. Refrigerate leftover fondue.

STOVETOP DIRECTIONS: Combine chocolate chips and light cream in heavy medium saucepan. Cook over low heat, stirring constantly, until chips are melted and mixture is hot. Stir in vanilla, and continue as in Step 2 above.

SPECIAL DARK® Fudge Fondue

## Chocolate Coconut Balls

*Makes about 4 dozen candies*

- 3 bars (1 ounce each) HERSHEY'S Unsweetened Baking Chocolate
- ¼ cup (½ stick) butter
- ½ cup sweetened condensed milk (not evaporated milk)
- ¾ cup granulated sugar
- ¼ cup water
- 1 tablespoon light corn syrup
- 1 teaspoon vanilla extract
- 2 cups MOUNDS® Sweetened Coconut Flakes
- 1 cup chopped nuts
  Powdered sugar

1. Melt chocolate and butter in large heavy saucepan over very low heat. Add sweetened condensed milk; stir to blend. Remove from heat.

2. Stir together granulated sugar, water and corn syrup in small saucepan. Cook over medium heat, stirring constantly, until sugar is dissolved. Cook, without stirring, until mixture reaches 250°F on candy thermometer or until a small amount of syrup, when dropped into very cold water, forms a firm ball which does not flatten when removed from water. (Bulb of candy thermometer should not rest on bottom of saucepan.) Remove from heat; stir into chocolate mixture. Add vanilla, coconut and nuts; stir until well blended.

3. Refrigerate about 1 hour or until firm enough to handle. Shape into 1-inch balls; roll in powdered sugar. Store tightly covered in cool, dry place.

NOTE: For best results, do not double this recipe.

## Chips and Bits Cookie Pie

*Makes 8 servings*

- ½ **cup (1 stick) butter or margarine, softened**
- 2 **eggs, beaten**
- 2 **teaspoons vanilla extract**
- 1 **cup sugar**
- ½ **cup all-purpose flour**
- 1 **cup HERSHEY'S Semi-Sweet Chocolate Chips**
- ½ **cup HEATH® BITS 'O BRICKLE® Almond Toffee Bits**
- ½ **cup chopped pecans or walnuts**
- 1 **unbaked (9-inch pie) crust**
  **Ice cream or whipped cream (optional)**

1. Heat oven to 350°F.

2. Beat butter with electric mixer on medium speed in large bowl until fluffy. Add eggs and vanilla; beat thoroughly. Stir together sugar and flour; add to butter mixture, mixing until well blended. Stir in chocolate chips, toffee bits and nuts; spread in unbaked pie crust.

3. Bake 45 to 50 minutes or until golden. Cool about 1 hour before serving; serve warm, or reheat cooled pie slices by microwaving on HIGH (100%) for about 10 seconds. Serve with ice cream or whipped cream, if desired.

## Chocolate Pecan Pie

*Makes 8 servings*

- 1 **cup sugar**
- ⅓ **cup HERSHEY'S Cocoa**
- 3 **eggs, lightly beaten**
- ¾ **cup light corn syrup**
- 1 **tablespoon butter or margarine, melted**
- 1 **teaspoon vanilla extract**
- 1 **cup pecan halves**
- 1 **unbaked (9-inch pie) crust**
  **Whipped topping (optional)**

1. Heat oven to 350°F.

2. Stir together sugar and cocoa in medium bowl. Add eggs, corn syrup, butter and vanilla; stir until well blended. Stir in pecans. Pour into unbaked pie crust.

3. Bake 60 minutes or until set. Remove to wire rack and cool completely. Garnish with whipped topping, if desired.

Chocolate Pecan Pie

## Classic Chocolate Cream Pie

*Makes 8 to 10 servings*

2½ bars (1 ounce each) HERSHEY'S Unsweetened Baking
  Chocolate, broken into pieces
3 cups milk, divided
1⅓ cups sugar
3 tablespoons all-purpose flour
3 tablespoons cornstarch
½ teaspoon salt
3 egg yolks
2 tablespoons butter or margarine
1½ teaspoons vanilla extract
1 baked (9-inch) pie crust, cooled, or 1 (9-inch) crumb crust
  Sweetened whipped cream (optional)

1. Combine chocolate and 2 cups milk in medium saucepan; cook over medium heat, stirring constantly, just until mixture boils. Remove from heat and set aside.

2. Stir together sugar, flour, cornstarch and salt in medium bowl. Whisk remaining 1 cup milk into egg yolks in separate bowl; stir into sugar mixture. Gradually add to chocolate mixture. Cook over medium heat, whisking constantly, until mixture boils; boil and stir 1 minute. Remove from heat; stir in butter and vanilla.

3. Pour into prepared crust; press plastic wrap directly onto surface. Cool; refrigerate until well chilled. Top with whipped cream, if desired.

Classic Chocolate Cream Pie

## Lighter Than Air Chocolate Delight

*Makes 8 servings*

 2 **envelopes unflavored gelatin**
 ½ **cup cold water**
 1 **cup boiling water**
 1⅓ **cups nonfat dry milk powder**
 ⅓ **cup HERSHEY'S Dutch Processed Cocoa or HERSHEY'S
     Cocoa**
 1 **tablespoon vanilla extract**
   **Dash salt**
   **Granulated sugar substitute to equal 14 teaspoons sugar**
 8 **large ice cubes**

**1.** Sprinkle gelatin over cold water in blender container; let stand
4 minutes to soften. Gently stir with rubber spatula, scraping gelatin
particles off sides; add boiling water to gelatin mixture. Cover; blend
until gelatin dissolves. Add milk powder, cocoa, vanilla and salt; blend
on medium speed until well mixed. Add sugar substitute and ice cubes;
blend on high speed until ice is crushed and mixture is smooth and fluffy.

**2.** Immediately pour into 4-cup mold. Cover; refrigerate until firm. Unmold
onto serving plate.

NOTE: Eight individual dessert dishes may be used in place of 4-cup
mold, if desired.

Lighter Than Air Chocolate Delight

## HERSHEY'S Premier White Chips Almond Fudge

*Makes about 3 dozen pieces or 1½ pounds fudge*

> 2 cups (12-ounce package) HERSHEY'S Premier White Chips
> ⅔ cup sweetened condensed milk (not evaporated milk)
> 1½ cups coarsely chopped slivered almonds, toasted*
> ½ teaspoon vanilla extract

*\*To toast almonds: Spread almonds in even layer on cookie sheet. Bake at 350°F for 8 to 10 minutes or until lightly browned, stirring occasionally; cool.*

1. Line 8-inch square pan with foil, extending foil over edges of pan.

2. Melt white chips with sweetened condensed milk in medium saucepan over very low heat, stirring constantly until mixture is smooth. Remove from heat. Stir in almonds and vanilla. Spread in prepared pan.

3. Cover; refrigerate 2 hours or until firm. Use foil to lift fudge out of pan; peel off foil. Cut fudge into squares.

NOTE: For best results, do not double this recipe.

HERSHEY'S Premier White Chips Almond Fudge

## SPECIAL DARK® Fudge Truffles

*Makes about 3 dozen truffles*

- 2 cups (12-ounce package) HERSHEY'S SPECIAL DARK® Chocolate Chips
- ¾ cup whipping cream
  Various coatings such as toasted chopped pecans, coconut, powdered sugar, cocoa or small candy pieces

1. Combine chocolate chips and whipping cream in medium microwave-safe bowl. Microwave at HIGH (100%) 1 minute; stir. If necessary, microwave an additional 15 seconds at a time, stirring after each heating, until chips are melted and mixture is smooth when stirred.

2. Refrigerate 3 hours or until firm. Shape mixture into 1-inch balls. Roll each ball in coating. Cover; store in refrigerator.

## Deep Dark Mousse

*Makes 4 to 6 servings*

- ¼ cup sugar
- 1 teaspoon unflavored gelatin
- ½ cup milk
- 1 cup HERSHEY'S SPECIAL DARK® Chocolate Chips
- 2 teaspoons vanilla extract
- 1 cup cold whipping cream
  Sweetened whipped cream (optional)

1. Stir together sugar and gelatin in small saucepan; stir in milk. Let stand 2 minutes to soften gelatin. Cook over medium heat, stirring constantly, until mixture just begins to boil.

2. Remove from heat. Immediately add chocolate chips; stir until melted. Stir in vanilla; cool to room temperature.

3. Beat whipping cream with electric mixer on medium speed in large bowl until stiff peaks form. Add half of chocolate mixture and gently fold until nearly combined; add remaining chocolate mixture and fold just until blended. Spoon into serving dish or individual dishes. Refrigerate. Garnish with sweetened whipped cream, if desired, just before serving.

## Toffee Popcorn Crunch

*Makes about 1 pound popcorn*

> 8 **cups popped popcorn**
> ¾ **cup whole or slivered almonds**
> 1⅓ **cups (8-ounce package) HEATH® BITS 'O BRICKLE®**
>     **Almond Toffee Bits**
> ½ **cup light corn syrup**

1. Heat oven to 275°F. Grease large roasting pan or two 13×9×2-inch baking pans. Place popcorn and almonds in prepared pan.

2. Combine toffee bits and corn syrup in heavy medium saucepan. Cook over medium heat, stirring constantly, until toffee melts (about 12 minutes). Pour over popcorn mixture; stir until evenly coated.

3. Bake 30 minutes, stirring frequently. Remove from oven; stir every 2 minutes until slightly cooled. Cool completely. Store in tightly covered container in cool, dry place.

NOTE: For best results, do not double this recipe.

# pies & desserts

## Milk Chocolate Pots de Crème

*Makes about 6 to 8 servings*

> 2 **cups (11½-ounce package) HERSHEY'S Milk Chocolate Chips**
> ½ **cup light cream**
> ½ **teaspoon vanilla extract**
> **Sweetened whipped cream (optional)**

**1.** Place milk chocolate chips and light cream in medium microwave-safe bowl. Microwave on HIGH (100%) 1 minute or just until chips are melted and mixture is smooth when stirred. Stir in vanilla.

**2.** Pour into demitasse cups or very small dessert dishes. Cover; refrigerate until firm. Serve cold with sweetened chipped cream, if desired.

## Hot Merry Mocha

*Makes about ten 6-ounce servings*

> 6 **tablespoons HERSHEY'S Cocoa**
> 1 **to 2 tablespoons powdered instant coffee**
> ⅛ **teaspoon salt**
> 6 **cups hot water**
> 1 **can (14 ounces) sweetened condensed milk (not evaporated milk)**
> **Sweetened whipped cream (optional)**

**1.** Stir together cocoa, instant coffee and salt in 4-quart saucepan; stir in water.

**2.** Cook over medium heat, stirring occasionally, until mixture boils. Stir in sweetened condensed milk. Heat thoroughly; do not boil. Beat with whisk until foamy. Serve hot, topped with sweetened whipped cream, if desired.

**VARIATION:** Minted Hot Chocolate: Follow directions above omitting instant coffee. Stir in ¼ to ½ teaspoon mint extract before beating. Serve with candy cane for stirrer, if desired.

Milk Chocolate Pots de Crème

## Butterscotch Nut Fudge

*Makes about 5 dozen pieces or about 2¼ pounds candy*

- 1¾  **cups sugar**
- 1  **jar (7 ounces) marshmallow creme**
- ¾  **cup evaporated milk**
- ¼  **cup (½ stick) butter**
- 1¾  **cups (11-ounce package) HERSHEY'S Butterscotch Chips**
- 1  **cup chopped salted mixed nuts**
- 1  **teaspoon vanilla extract**

1. Line 8-inch square pan with foil, extending foil over edges of pan.

2. Combine sugar, marshmallow creme, evaporated milk and butter in heavy 3-quart saucepan. Cook over medium heat, stirring constantly, until mixture comes to full boil; boil and stir 5 minutes.

3. Remove from heat; gradually add butterscotch chips, stirring until chips are melted. Stir in nuts and vanilla. Pour into prepared pan; cool.

4. Refrigerate 2 to 3 hours. Remove from pan; place on cutting board. Peel off foil. Cut into squares. Store tightly covered in refrigerator.

# index

# notes

# METRIC CONVERSION CHART

## VOLUME MEASUREMENTS (dry)

$1/8$ teaspoon = 0.5 mL
$1/4$ teaspoon = 1 mL
$1/2$ teaspoon = 2 mL
$3/4$ teaspoon = 4 mL
1 teaspoon = 5 mL
1 tablespoon = 15 mL
2 tablespoons = 30 mL
$1/4$ cup = 60 mL
$1/3$ cup = 75 mL
$1/2$ cup = 125 mL
$2/3$ cup = 150 mL
$3/4$ cup = 175 mL
1 cup = 250 mL
2 cups = 1 pint = 500 mL
3 cups = 750 mL
4 cups = 1 quart = 1 L

## VOLUME MEASUREMENTS (fluid)

1 fluid ounce (2 tablespoons) = 30 mL
4 fluid ounces ($1/2$ cup) = 125 mL
8 fluid ounces (1 cup) = 250 mL
12 fluid ounces ($1 1/2$ cups) = 375 mL
16 fluid ounces (2 cups) = 500 mL

## WEIGHTS (mass)

$1/2$ ounce = 15 g
1 ounce = 30 g
3 ounces = 90 g
4 ounces = 120 g
8 ounces = 225 g
10 ounces = 285 g
12 ounces = 360 g
16 ounces = 1 pound = 450 g

## DIMENSIONS

$1/16$ inch = 2 mm
$1/8$ inch = 3 mm
$1/4$ inch = 6 mm
$1/2$ inch = 1.5 cm
$3/4$ inch = 2 cm
1 inch = 2.5 cm

## OVEN TEMPERATURES

250°F = 120°C
275°F = 140°C
300°F = 150°C
325°F = 160°C
350°F = 180°C
375°F = 190°C
400°F = 200°C
425°F = 220°C
450°F = 230°C

## BAKING PAN SIZES

| Utensil | Size in Inches/Quarts | Metric Volume | Size in Centimeters |
|---|---|---|---|
| Baking or Cake Pan (square or rectangular) | $8 \times 8 \times 2$ | 2 L | $20 \times 20 \times 5$ |
| | $9 \times 9 \times 2$ | 2.5 L | $23 \times 23 \times 5$ |
| | $12 \times 8 \times 2$ | 3 L | $30 \times 20 \times 5$ |
| | $13 \times 9 \times 2$ | 3.5 L | $33 \times 23 \times 5$ |
| Loaf Pan | $8 \times 4 \times 3$ | 1.5 L | $20 \times 10 \times 7$ |
| | $9 \times 5 \times 3$ | 2 L | $23 \times 13 \times 7$ |
| Round Layer Cake Pan | $8 \times 1 1/2$ | 1.2 L | $20 \times 4$ |
| | $9 \times 1 1/2$ | 1.5 L | $23 \times 4$ |
| Pie Plate | $8 \times 1 1/4$ | 750 mL | $20 \times 3$ |
| | $9 \times 1 1/4$ | 1 L | $23 \times 3$ |
| Baking Dish or Casserole | 1 quart | 1 L | — |
| | $1 1/2$ quart | 1.5 L | — |
| | 2 quart | 2 L | — |